For Better
And
For Worse

Selected by
Bruce Lansky

Meadowbrook Press

Distributed by Simon & Schuster
New York

Library of Congress Cataloging-in-Publication Data

For better and for worse: the best quotes about marriage / Selected by Bruce Lansky.

      p.   cm.

Originally published 1995.

Includes index.

ISBN: 0-88166-291-7 (Meadowbrook)

ISBN: 0-671-52122-5 (Simon & Schuster)

1. Marriage—Quotations, maxims, etc.   I. Lansky, Bruce.

PN6084.M3F67 1997

306.81—dc21   96-29458

                                CIP

Editor: Bruce Lansky

Editorial Coordinator: Craig Hansen and Steven Roe

Cartoon Editor: Steven Roe

Production Manager: Joe Gagne

Production Assistant: Danielle White

Cover Design: Nancy Tuminelly

Cover Illustrator: Jack Lindstrom

© 1997 by Meadowbrook Creations

Quotes: p. 69 from Eric W. Johnson, *A Treasury of Humor: An Indexed Collection of Anecdotes* (Prometheus Books; Amherst, NY). © 1989 by Prometheus Books. Reprinted with permission of the publisher.

Poems: p. 40 "To Keep your marriage brimming . . ." by Ogden Nash. From *Verses from 1929 On*. © 1962 by Ogden Nash. By permission of Little, Brown, and Company; p.40 "He drinks because she scolds, he thinks . . ." by Ogden Nash. From *Verses from 1929 On*. © 1962 by Ogden Nash. By permission of Little, Brown, and Company.

Published by Meadowbrook Press, 5451 Smetana Drive, Minnetonka, MN 55343

BOOK TRADE DISTRIBUTION by Simon & Schuster, a division of Simon and Schuster, Inc., 1230 Avenue of the Americas, New York, NY 10020

00 99 98 97   10 9 8 7 6 5 4 3 2 1

Printed in the United States of America

CONTENTS

Introduction v
Still Single 1
Getting Married 3
Weddings 13
Wives 18
Husbands 25
In-Laws 37
Communication 40
Love 48
Sex 53
Married with Children 60
Domestic Life 63
For Better and for Worse 70
Anniversaries 77
Battle of the Sexes 78
Bickering 86
Fighting 87
Cheating 90
Divorce 96
Remarriage 100
Till Death Do Us Part 102
Index 104

ACKNOWLEDGMENTS

We would like to thank the individuals who served
on the reading panel for this project:

Elizabeth Bolton, Cathy Broberg, Dorothy Brummel, Gail Clark, Faye Click,
Charles Ghigna, Babs Bell Hajdusiewicz, Karen Hammond, Dick Hayman, Joan
Horton, Laura Irvin, Jo S. Kittinger, Ann Lynch, Sydnie Meltzer Kleinhenz, Kim
and Todd Koehler, Janet McCann, Ingrid McCleary, Charlene Meltzer, Barbara
Merchant, Mrs. Rolaine M. Merchant, Robin Michel, Ruth Moose, Lois Muehl,
Sheryl Nelms, Elaine Nick, Jeanne Nelson, Joi Nobisso, Elizabeth Paterra, Claire
Puneky, Lori Reed, Heidi Roemer, Jerry Rosen, Rita Schlachter, Rosemary
Schmidt, Pattie Schnetzler, Robert Scotellaro, Mary Scott, Nancy Sweetland,
Janet Thomas, Esther Towns, Penny Warner, Vicki Wiita,
and C. Pleasants York

INTRODUCTION

I love collecting funny quotes and sharing them with friends. It's fun to watch smiles creep across their faces and to listen to their laughter. What's most interesting is that after smiling or laughing, they often say, "That's so true!"

What's fun about the love and marriage quotes I've collected is discovering that someone had the same experience, perception, or thought that you did—and wrote it down.

For example, on the subject of getting married, John Louis Anderson wrote, "The big problem with living in sin is that nobody rewards that kind of behavior with gifts." This thought occurred to me, but I never wrote it down.

I hope you find these quotes as entertaining as I do. But to the extent that these quotes reveal some of the "truth" about relationships, I think they'll provide engaged couples and newlyweds with a perspective on the "better" and the "worse" of married life. And they will remind "oldlyweds," as well as those who are separated or divorced, that they're not alone in dealing with the inevitable ups and downs of relationships.

Bruce Lansky

I think; therefore, I'm single.
—*Lizz Winstead*

I never married because there was no need.
I have three pets at home that answer
the same purpose as a husband.
I have a dog that growls every morning,
a parrot that swears all afternoon,
and a cat that comes home late at night.
—*Marie Corelli*

I've never been married,
but I tell people I'm divorced so they
won't think something's wrong with me.
—*Elayne Boosler*

Marriage is a great institution,
but I'm not ready for an institution yet.
—*Mae West*

Marriage is a wonderful invention;
but, then again, so is a bicycle repair kit.
—*Billy Connolly*

Wanted: a good woman who can clean, cook fish, dig worms, sew, and who owns a good fishing boat and motor. Please enclose photo of boat and motor!
—*Dave Haught*

I joined a singles group in my neighborhood. The other day the president called me up and said, "Welcome to the group. I want to find out what kind of activities you like to plan." I said, "Well, weddings."
—*Lynn Harris*

Out to lunch. Think it over.
—sign on the door of a
marriage license bureau

The big problem with living in sin is that nobody rewards that kind of behavior with gifts.
—John Louis Anderson

It's a funny thing that when a man hasn't got anything on earth to worry about, he goes off and gets married.
—Robert Frost

You know what I did before I married?
Anything I wanted to.
—*Henny Youngman*

One of the best things about marriage
is that it gets young people to bed
at a decent hour.
—*M. M. Musselman*

One good reason to get married is
you'll always have someone to blame
when you can't find your keys.
—*John Louis Anderson*

"By the power vested in me by the state of New York, I hereby pronounce you two living together. Tom, you may now kiss your roommate."

I think men who have a pierced ear
are better prepared for marriage.
They've experienced pain and bought jewelry.
—*Rita Rudner*

When I was young, I vowed never to marry
until I found the ideal woman.
Well, I found her—but, alas,
she was waiting for the ideal man.
—*Robert Schumann*

Whenever you want to marry someone,
go have lunch with his ex-wife.
—*Shelly Winters*

Never marry a widow
whose first husband was poisoned.
—*Gladiola Montana and Texas Bix Bender*

Never marry a man who refers to the
rehearsal dinner as "The Last Supper."
—*Diana Jordan and Paul Seaburn*

Don't marry a man to reform him—
that's what reform schools are for.
—*Mae West*

My wife and I were happy for
twenty years. Then we met.
—*Rodney Dangerfield*

If you want to sacrifice the admiration
of many men for the criticism of one,
go ahead, get married.
—*Katharine Hepburn*

I saw my friend the other day and
she had her wedding ring on the wrong finger.
When I pointed this out to her, she said,
"I know, I married the wrong man."
—*Susan Savannah*

A successful man is one who makes more money than his wife can spend. A successful woman is one who can find such a man.
—*Lana Turner*

I want a man who's kind and understanding. Is that too much to ask of a millionaire?
—*Zsa Zsa Gabor*

Two people can live as cheaply as one. For half as long.
—*Anonymous*

The trouble with some women is
that they get all excited about nothing—
and then marry him.
—Cher

Marrying a man is like having
your hair cut short. You won't know
whether it suits you until it's too late.
—Jane Goodsell

Gettin' married's like getting into a tub
of hot water. After you get used to it,
it ain't so hot.
—Minnie Pearl

By all means, marry; if you get a good wife,
you'll be happy. If you get a bad one,
you'll become a philosopher.
—*Socrates*

If you marry, you will regret it; if you do not
marry, you will also regret it.
—*Soren Kierkegaard*

I never knew what real happiness was
until I got married. And by then,
it was too late.
—*Max Kaufman*

I married the first man I ever kissed.
When I tell my children that,
they just about throw up.
—*Barbara Bush*

Your spouse should be just attractive enough
to turn you on. Anything more is trouble.
—*Albert Brooks*

Marriage: the arrangement before
the arraignment.
—*Babs Bell Hajdusiewicz*

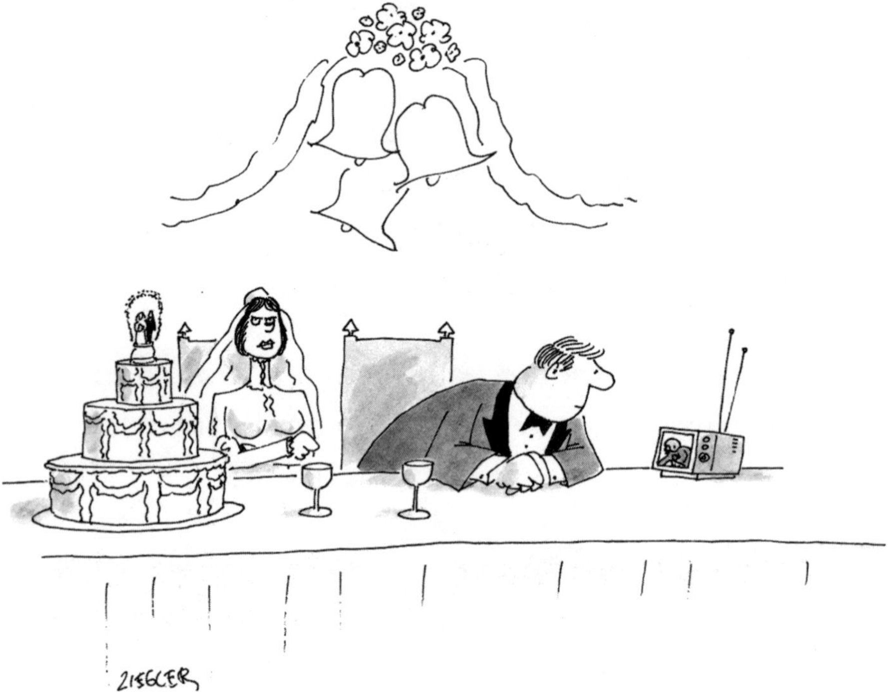
ZIEGLER

Keep your eyes wide open before marriage,
half shut afterwards.
—*Benjamin Franklin*

I told someone I was getting married,
and they said, "Have you picked a date yet?"
I said, "Wow, you can bring a date to
your own wedding?" What a country!
—*Yakov Smirnoff*

My cousin just got married for the totally
wrong reasons. She married a man for money.
She wasn't real subtle about it.
Instead of calling him her fiancé,
she kept calling him her financee.
—*Rita Rudner*

The wedding is a beautiful thing.
I think the idea behind the tuxedo
is the woman's point of view that
"Men are all the same, we might as well
dress them that way."
—*Jerry Seinfeld*

I was the best man at the wedding.
If I'm the best man,
why is she marrying him?
—*Jerry Seinfeld*

I was married by a judge.
I should have asked for a jury.
—*George Burns*

Why did the Emperor have no clothes?
His wife had been out of town for a week.
—*Cindy Garner*

Why do men like to marry women
who remind them of their mothers?
Who else would put up with them?
—*Cindy Garner*

But let a woman in your life
And your serenity is through!
She'll redecorate your home
From the cellar to the dome;
Then get on to the enthralling
Fun of overhauling
You.
—*Alan Jay Lerner*

Basically, my wife was immature.
I'd be at home in the bath, and she'd
come in and sink my boats.
—*Woody Allen*

My wife thinks I'm nosy. At least that's what
she keeps scribbling in her diary.
—*Drake Sather*

My wife is really sentimental.
One Valentine's Day I gave her a ring,
and to this day, she has never forgotten
those three little words that were
engraved inside—*Made in Taiwan!*
—*Leopold Fetchner*

Some wives can cook, but don't.
My wife can't cook, but does.
—*Henny Youngman*

My wife dresses to kill.
She cooks the same way.
—*Henny Youngman*

"I know you're going to love this!
The Surgeon General's Office said it's bad for you."

Do you know what it means to come home at
night to a woman who'll give you a little love,
a little affection, and a little tenderness?
It means you're in the wrong house.
—*Henny Youngman*

A man likes his wife to be just clever enough
to comprehend his cleverness,
and just stupid enough to admire it.
—*Israel Zangwill*

The wife who enjoys being put on a pedestal
usually objects to being put on a scale.
—*Evan Esar*

Happy the man with a wife to tell him
what to do and a secretary
to do it for him.
—Lord Mancroft

A good wife always forgives her husband
when she's wrong.
—Milton Berle

A wife is a person who can look in the
top drawer of a dresser and find a man's
handkerchief that isn't there.
—Lou Apuzzo

If you want to be loved
for the rest of your life,
be more of a woman
and less of a wife.
—Susan D. Anderson

An ideal wife is one who remains faithful
to you but tries to be just as charming
as if she weren't.
—Sacha Guitry

Why can't a woman be more like a man?
Men are so honest, so thoroughly square;
Eternally noble, historically fair;
Who when you win will always give your back a pat—
Why can't a woman be like that?
—Alan Jay Lerner

Whose duty is it to see that I am
well cared for? Oh, I would love a wife.
—*Judy Blume*

I have yet to hear a man ask for advice
on how to combine marriage and a career.
—*Gloria Steinem*

Women are more verbal than men. That's why
when you see an eldlerly couple together, it's
always the man who has the hearing aid.
—*Jeff Stilson*

My husband is a know-it-all.
I finally had to tell him,
"When I want your opinion,
I'll tell you what it is."
—*Charlene Meltzer*

Never give your husband an idea
he can't pretend was his to begin with.
—*Susan D. Anderson*

The best way to get most husbands
to do something is to suggest
that perhaps they're too old to do it.
—*Ann Bancroft*

The male is a domestic animal who,
if treated with firmness and kindness,
can be trained to do most things.
—*Jilly Cooper*

Any husband who says,
"My wife and I are completely equal partners,"
is talking about either a law firm
or a hand of bridge.
—*Bill Cosby*

A man's home may seem to be his castle on the
outside; inside it is more often his nursery.
—*Clare Luce Booth*

"I wish someone would take him out to the ballgame and leave him there."

Husbands think we should know where
everything is. He asks me, "Roseanne,
do we have any Cheetos left?" Like he can't
go over to that sofa cushion
and lift it himself.
—*Roseanne*

I can always find my husband.
I just follow his trail of dirty clothes.
—*Babs Bell Hajdusiewicz*

A smart husband buys his wife very fine china
so she won't trust him to wash it.
—*Leopold Fetchner*

Your husband is always out of town when
the furnace breaks down, the lawn needs
mowing, the sink starts leaking,
or the package from Victoria's Secret
finally arrives.
—*Bruce Lansky*

More husbands would leave home
if they knew how to pack their suitcases.
—*Leopold Fetchner*

Husbands are like fires.
They go out if unattended.
—*Zsa Zsa Gabor*

There is so little difference between husbands;
you might as well keep the first.
—*Adela Rodgers St. Johns*

All husbands are alike,
but they have different faces
so you can tell them apart.
—*Lawrence J. Peters*

My husband says he wants to spend his
vacation someplace where
he's never been before.
I said, "How about the kitchen?"
—*Nan Tucket*

"*Stan Freebish has an automatic dishwasher, . . . Mel Dister
has an automatic dishwasher, . . . Harry Blipsik has . . .*"

Women who think of their husbands
as angels are widows.
—*Bruce Lansky*

A husband is a person who expects his wife
to be perfect and to understand why he isn't.
—*Anonymous*

My husband has a good head
on his shoulders—mine.
—*Babs Bell Hajdusiewicz*

Just be considerate, accept each other
for what you are, and don't point out
that the hair he's losing on his head is now
growing out of his nose—and his ears.
—*Peg Bundy on* Married . . . with Children

What's the difference between a boyfriend
and a husband? About 30 pounds.
—*Cindy Garner*

You never see a man walking down the
street with a woman who has a pot belly
and a bald spot.
—*Elayne Boosler*

In August, my husband, Morris, and I celebrated our 38th wedding anniversary. You know what I finally realized? If I had killed the man the first time I thought about it, I'd have been out of jail by now.

—*Anita Milner*

Men have a much better time of it than women; for one thing, they marry later; for another thing, they die earlier.

—*H.L. Mencken*

I haven't spoken to my mother-in-law
for eighteen months—
I don't like to interrupt her.
—*Ken Dodd*

Behind every successful man
stands a surprised mother-in-law.
—*Hubert H. Humphrey*

Adam was lucky. He had no mother-in-law.
—*Sholem Aleichem*

"We located the hissing noise, Mr. Watkins. Your wife's mother is in the back seat."

I told my mother-in-law that my house
was her house, and she said,
"Get the hell off my property."
—*Joan Rivers*

Be kind to your mother-in-law.
Baby sitters are expensive!
—*Leopold Fetchner*

I sent my mother-in-law a present
on Mother's Day—her daughter.
—*Henny Youngman*

To keep your marriage brimming,
With love in the loving cup,
Whenever you're wrong, admit it;
Whenever you're right, shut up.
—*Ogden Nash*

He drinks because she scolds, he thinks;
She thinks she scolds because he drinks;
And neither will admit what's true,
That he's a sot and she's a shrew.
—*Ogden Nash*

I can't get along with my wife—
she understands me.
—*Henny Youngman*

The only thing that holds a marriage together
is the husband being big enough to step back
and see where the wife is wrong.
—*Archie Bunker*

Before marriage, a man declares
he would lay down his life to serve you;
after marriage, he won't even lay down
his paper to talk to you.
—*Helen Rowland*

The husband who doesn't tell his wife
everything probably reasons that what she
doesn't know won't hurt him.
—*Leo J. Burke*

Before marriage, a man will lie awake
all night thinking about something you said;
after marriage, he will fall asleep
before you have finished saying it.
—*Helen Rowland*

I miss married life.
I haven't had a good argument in years.
—*Bruce Lansky*

What's the difference between
the average man and E.T.?
E.T. phoned home.
—*Cindy Garner*

The same time that women came up with PMS,
men came up with ESPN.
—*Blake Clark*

When women are depressed,
they either eat or go shopping.
Men invade another country.
It's a whole different way of thinking.
—*Elayne Boosler*

Only two things are necessary to keep
one's wife happy. One is to let her think
she is having her own way, and the other
is to let her have it.
—*Lyndon B. Johnson*

My wife thinks it's romantic
the way our neighbor kisses his wife good-bye
every morning at the front door.
She said, "Why don't you do that?"
I replied, "I don't even know her name!"
—*Bruce Lansky*

Your marriage is in trouble if your wife
says, "You're only interested in one thing,"
and you can't remember what it is.
—*Milton Berle*

Opinions expressed
By the man in this house
Should not be confused
With those held by his spouse.
—*Susan D. Anderson*

She lied to me. She told me that
her father was a banker, and his health
was failing. After the marriage,
I found out his health was fine.
It was the bank that was failing.
—*Milton Berle*

All men make mistakes, but married men
find out about them sooner.
—*Red Skelton*

"True love," like "living happily ever after," can mainly be found in the pages of fairy tales.
—*Bruce Lansky*

Husband: "Darling, will you love me when I'm old and feeble?"
Wife: "Of course I do."
—*H. Alan Dunn*

If you want to read about love and marriage, you've got to buy two separate books.
—*Alan King*

Love may be blind,
but marriage is a real eye opener.
—*Bruce Lansky*

Before I met my husband,
I'd never fallen in love,
though I'd stepped in it a few times.
—*Rita Rudner*

"I'm already hopelessly in love with a married man—my husband."

I love being married. . . . It's so great to find
that one special person you want to annoy
for the rest of your life.
—*Rita Rudner*

You always nag the one you love.
—*Bruce Lansky*

Love: a temporary insanity
curable by marriage.
—*Ambrose Bierce*

The first part of our marriage was
very happy. But then, on the way back
from the ceremony . . .
—*Henny Youngman*

I know a lot of people didn't expect
our relationship to last—but we've just
celebrated our two months' anniversary.
—*Britt Ekland*

The best aphrodisiac is making up
after a good fight.
—*Sydnie Meltzer Kleinhenz*

Oysters are supposed to
enhance your sexual performance,
but they don't work for me.
Maybe I put them on too soon.
—*Garry Shandling*

The secret of being a good lover
is not knowing when to stop.
—*Ashleigh Brilliant*

During sex, my wife wants to talk to me.
The other night she called me from a hotel.
—*Rodney Dangerfield*

I don't see much of Alfred anymore,
since he got so interested in sex.
—*Mrs. Alfred Kinsey*

Sex when you're married is like going to a
7-Eleven. There's not as much variety, but at
three in the morning it's always there.
—*Carol Leifer*

**Nothing was happening in my marriage.
I nicknamed our waterbed "Lake Placid."**
—*Phyllis Diller*

**We practice safe sex. We gave up
the chandelier a long time ago.**
—*Kathy Lee Gifford*

My wife and I have a great relationship.
I love sex, and she'll *do* anything
to get out of the kitchen.
—*Milton Berle*

My husband makes love to me
almost every day of the week—almost Monday,
almost Tuesday, almost Wednesday . . .
—*Ruth Berle*

The other night I said to my wife, Ruth,
"Do you feel that sex and excitement
have gone out of our marriage?"
Ruth said, "I'll discuss it with you
during the next commercial."
—*Milton Berle*

"As long as we're in bed, why don't we go to sleep."

Both of my ex-wives closed their eyes
when making love, because they didn't
want to see me having a good time.
—*Joseph Wambaugh*

If God wanted sex to be fun, He wouldn't
have included children as a punishment.
—*Ed Bluestone*

Snuggle: an act of warmth that your husband
will inevitably interpret as foreplay.
—*Tom Carey*

My husband is German;
every night I get dressed up like Poland
and he invades me.
—*Bette Midler*

Women complain about sex more than men.
Their gripes fall into two major categories:
1. Not enough
2. Too much
—*Ann Landers*

"Your father and I want to explain why we've decided to live apart."

Children are nature's very own form
of birth control.
—*Dave Barry*

My husband and I found this great new method
of birth control that really, really works. . . .
Every night before we go to bed, we spend
an hour with our kids.
—*Roseanne*

Contestant: "I am the father of ten children."
Groucho Marx: "Why so many children?"
Contestant: "Well, I love my wife."
Groucho Marx: "I love my cigar, but I take it out
of my mouth once in a while."
—*You Bet Your Life* TV show

Ours is an old-fashioned family;
my husband, the children, and I
all have the same phone number.
—*Jean H. Marvin*

Nine words often heard on second
honeymoons: "What do you think
the kids are doing now?"
—*Linda Fiterman*

Marriage lowers your phone bill—
until you have teenagers.
—*Lois Muehl*

That shows how long we've been married. Now you kiss me to calm me down.
—*Bette Davis*

After twenty-seven years of marriage, my wife and I have finally achieved sexual compatibility. Now we get simultaneous headaches.
—*Clifforn Kuhn*

There's no question that sometimes the romance does go out of a marriage. If you've been married twenty-five years, foreplay is a nudge.
—*Robert Orben*

I hate housework! You make the beds,
you do the dishes—and six months later
you have to start all over again.
—*Joan Rivers*

As a housewife, I feel that if the kids are
still alive when my husband gets home from
work, then hey, I've done my job.
—*Roseanne*

How many men does it take
to change a roll of toilet paper?
We don't know. It never happened.
—*Nan Tucket*

Some people ask the secret of our long marriage. We take time to go to a restaurant two times a week. A little candlelight, dinner, soft music, and dancing. She goes Tuesdays, I go Fridays.

—*Henny Youngman*

I bought my wife a new car. She called me and said, "There was water in the carburetor." I said, "Where's the car?" She said, "In the lake."

—*Henny Youngman*

Married men want to find dinner
on the table when they get home.
So do married women.
—*Bruce Lansky*

"What's for supper, Dear!"

Who wears the pants in this house?
I do, and I also wash and iron them.
—*Dennis Thatcher, Margaret's husband*

Why does a woman work for years
to change a man's habits,
and then complain that he's not
the man she married?
—*Barbra Streisand*

As Alicia was getting to know Michael and his family, she was very impressed by how much his parents loved each other.

"They're so thoughtful," Alicia said. "Why, your dad even brings your mom a cup of hot coffee in bed in the morning."

After a time, Alicia and Michael were engaged, and then married. On the way from the wedding to the reception, Alicia again remarked on Michael's loving parents, and even the coffee in bed. "Tell me," she said, "does it run in the family?"

"It sure does," replied Michael, "and I take after my mom."

—*Eric W. Johnson*

Marriage: a period during which a man
finds out what sort of fellow his wife
would have preferred.
—*The Vagabonds*

Marriage is not merely sharing fettuccini,
but sharing the burden of finding the fettuccini
restaurant in the first place.
—*Calvin Trillin*

Marriage is a woman's hair net tangled in a
man's spectacles on top of a dresser drawer.
—*Don Herold*

Marriage is the alliance of two people,
one of whom never remembers birthdays
and the other who never forgets them.
—*Ogden Nash*

A good marriage would be between
a blind wife and a deaf husband.
—*Montaigne*

"Honey, relax. I can explain everything."

You're handsome and funny,
You're charming and kind,
Your body is stunning,
And so is your mind.

Your talents are many,
Your wardrobe is great,
But nothing surpasses
Your taste in a mate.

—*Ellen Jackson*

Marriage is an alliance entered into by a man
who can't sleep with the window shut, and a
woman who can't sleep with the window open.
—*George Bernard Shaw*

The spouse who snores loudest
always falls asleep first.
—*Bruce Lansky*

You know when your honeymoon is over?
It's when the dog brings your slippers
and your wife barks at you.
—*Roy Bolitho*

The honeymoon is over when he phones that
he'll be late for supper—and she has already
left a note that it's in the refrigerator.
—*Bill Lawrence*

Marriage is like paying an endless visit
in your worst clothes.
—*J.B. Priestley*

The more soap operas you watch on TV,
the better your own marriage looks.
—*Bruce Lansky*

Anniversaries were invented to give
husbands a day to forget something
other than their wives' birthdays.
—*Craig Hansen*

What's the best way to have your husband
remember your anniversary?
Get married on his birthday.
—*Cindy Garner*

What's the worst thing you could get on
your twenty-fifth wedding anniversary?
Morning sickness.
—*Nan Tucket*

For two people in a marriage to live
together day after day is unquestionably
the one miracle that the Vatican
has overlooked.
—Bill Cosby

My parents stayed together for forty years,
but that was out of spite.
—Woody Allen

Marriage is the only war where
one sleeps with the enemy.
—Anonymous

"Couldn't you at least wait until halftime, so we can discuss our communication problem?"

Adam and Eve were doing fine until they started worrying about what to wear.
—*Monica and Bill Dodds*

You know your marriage is in trouble when your current husband introduces you to people as his "first wife."
—*Linda Fiterman*

Any man today who returns from work, sinks into a chair, and calls for his pipe is a man with an appetite for danger.
—*Bill Cosby*

If I didn't understand you so well,
I wouldn't disagree with you so much.
—*Ashleigh Brilliant*

I'm so unlucky. I have a collie, a fox terrier,
and a poodle—and the only one
who barks at me is my wife.
—*Robert Orben*

We sleep in separate rooms,
we have dinner apart,
we take separate vacations—
we're doing everything we can
to keep our marriage together.
—*Rodney Dangerfield*

I grew up in a very large family
in a very small house.
I never slept alone
until after I was married.
—*Lewis Grizzard*

Men and women, women and men:
It will never work.
—*Erica Jong*

Marriage is life's way of proving
how opposite the opposite sex can be.
—*John Louis Anderson*

Marriage is like a besieged fortress.
Everyone outside wants to get in, and
everyone inside wants to get out.
—*Quitard*

"Good morning, beheaded—uh, I mean beloved."

Lady Aster: "If you were my husband,
I'd put poison in your tea."
Churchill: "Madam, if you were my wife,
I'd drink it."
—*Roger Bates*

In our family, we don't divorce our men—
we bury them.
—*Ruth Gordon*

Aren't they a lovely couple? He's willing to
die for her, and she's willing to let him.
—*Leopold Fetchner*

I wouldn't object to my wife having the last word—if only she'd get to it.
—*Henny Youngman*

My wife gave me a wonderful birthday present. She let me win an argument.
—*Leopold Fetchner*

Never go to bed mad. Stay up and fight.
—*Phyllis Diller*

My wife and I had a rather interesting fight last night. She said it was five days since our last fight—and I said it was four.
—*Robert Orben*

When a man brings his wife flowers for no reason—there's a reason.
—*Molly McGee*

The best thing about being married with
children is you always have a referee.
—*Babs Bell Hajdusiewicz*

If it weren't for marriage, men and women
would have to fight with total strangers.
—*Anonymous*

My husband said he needed more space,
so I locked him outside.
—*Roseanne*

I know a fellow who wants to get married,
but he can't. He's a pacifist.
—*Robert Orben*

My mother buried three husbands,
and two of them were just napping.
—*Rita Rudner*

Monogamy is the Western custom of
one wife and hardly any mistresses.
—*H.H. Munro ("Saki")*

Woman wants monogamy;
Man delights in novelty. . . .
With this the gist and sum of it,
What earthly good can come of it?
—*Dorothy Parker*

Some people actually cheat on the people they're cheating with, which is like holding up a bank and then turning to the robber next to you and going, "All right, give me everything you got, too."
—*Jerry Seinfeld*

While in bed with her husband's best friend, a woman got a phone call. "That was Sam, but don't worry. He won't be home for a while. He's playing cards with you."
—*Susan Savannah*

I told my wife the truth. I told her I was seeing a psychiatrist. Then she told me the truth: that she was seeing a psychiatrist, two plumbers, and a bartender.
—*Rodney Dangerfield*

I've been in love with the same woman for forty-one years. If my wife finds out, she'll kill me.
—*Henny Youngman*

In some countries, being president is just an honorary position— like being a husband in Hollywood.
—*Earl Wilson*

*"I'm sorry your wife doesn't understand you and yes,
I'll be happy to see you sometime. Bring your wife along.
I'm a marriage counselor."*

When a man steals your wife, there is no better revenge than to let him keep her.
—Sacha Guitry

My wife doesn't care what I do when I'm away, as long as I don't have a good time.
—Lee Trevino

My husband will never chase another woman. He's too fine, too decent, too old.
—Gracie Allen

Eighty percent of married men cheat in
America. The rest cheat in Europe.
—*Jackie Mason*

Do you know what the rate of literacy is
in the United States? Eighty-six percent.
Do you know how many married people have
committed adultery? Eighty-seven percent.
This is the only country in the world that has
more cheaters than readers.
—*Neil Simon*

An old lady stopped me on the street.
She says, "Johnny, I want a divorce from you."
And I say, "But we're not married." She says,
"Yeah, but I want to skip right to the goodies."
—*Johnny Carson*

You may think that my giving advice on marriage
is like the captain of the Titanic giving lessons
on navigation.
—*Johnny Carson*

Instead of getting married again, I'm going to find a woman I don't like and give her a house.
—*Lewis Grizzard*

Alimony is like putting gas into another guy's car.
—*Milton Berle*

I am a marvelous housekeeper.
Every time I leave a man, I keep his house.
—*Zsa Zsa Gabor*

"He didn't exactly ask for a divorce—he offered me an early-retirement package."

Easy divorces have just about put arguing
out of business.
—*Red Skelton*

Our eighteen-month trial separation
had gone so well, we decided to
make it permanent.
—*John Cleese*

Statistics prove that the leading cause
of divorce is marriage.
—*Bruce Lansky*

I'm the only man who has a marriage license made out, "To Whom It May Concern."
—*Mickey Rooney*

Marriage is a lot like the army: everyone complains, but you'd be surprised at the large number that reenlist.
—*James Garner*

"*Dearly beloved, we are gathered here yet again . . .*"

The secret of a happy marriage
remains a secret.
—*Henny Youngman*

People are always asking couples whose marriages
have endured at least a quarter of a century
for their secret for success. Actually, it is no secret
at all. I am a forgiving woman. Long ago, I forgave my
husband for not being Paul Newman.
—*Erma Bombeck*

Sigmund Freud once said, "What do women want?"
The only thing I have learned in fifty-two years
is that women want men to stop asking dumb
questions like that.
—*Bill Cosby*

The best thing that can happen to a couple married for fifty years or more is that they both grow nearsighted together.
—*Linda Fiterman*

An archaeologist is the best husband a woman can have; the older she gets, the more interested he is in her.
—*Agatha Christie*

I've been married so long, I'm on my third bottle of Tabasco sauce.
—*Susan Vass*

INDEX

Aleichem, Sholem, 37
Allen, Gracie, 94
Allen, Woody, 19, 78
Anderson, John Louis, 4, 5, 83
Anderson, Susan D., 24, 26, 47
Anonymous, 4, 10, 34, 78, 88
Apuzzo, Lou, 23
Bancroft, Ann, 26
Barry, Dave, 61
Bates, Roger, 85
Bender, Texas Bix and Gladiola Montana, 8
Berle, Milton, 23, 46, 47, 56, 97
Berle, Ruth, 56
Bierce, Ambrose, 52
Bluestone, Ed, 58
Blume, Judy, 25
Bolitho, Roy, 75
Bombeck, Erma, 102
Boosler, Elayne, 2, 35, 44
Booth, Clare Luce, 27
Booth, George, 38
Brilliant, Ashleigh, 53, 81
Brooks, Albert, 13

Bundy, Peg, on Married . . . with Children, 35
Bunker, Archie, 41
Burke, Leo J., 42
Burns, George, 17
Bush, Barbara, 13
Carey, Tom, 59
Carson, Johnny, 96
Cher, 11
Christie, Agatha, 103
Clark, Blake, 44
Cleese, John, 99
Connolly, Billy, 2
Cooper, Jilly, 27
Corelli, Marie, 1
Cosby, Bill, 27, 78, 80, 102
Dangerfield, Rodney, 9, 54, 82, 92
Davis, Bette, 63
Diller, Phyllis, 55, 87
Dodd, Ken, 37
Dodds, Monica and Bill, 80
Dunn, H. Alan, 48
Ekland, Britt, 52
Esar, Evan, 22
Farris, Joseph, vi, 50, 93
Fetchner, Leopold, 19, 30, 39, 85, 86

Fischer, Ed. 45
Fiterman, Linda, 62, 80, 103
Fradon, Dana, 84
Franklin, Benjamin, 15
Frost, Robert, 4
Gabor, Zsa Zsa, 10, 31, 97
Garner, Cindy, 18, 35, 43, 77
Garner, James, 100
Gerberg, Mort, 98
Gifford, Kathy Lee, 55
Goodsell, Jane, 11
Gordon, Ruth, 85
Grizzard, Lewis, 82, 97
Guitry, Sacha, 24, 94
Hajdusiewicz, Babs Bell, 13, 29, 34, 88
Hansen, Craig, 77
Harris, Lynn, 3
Haught, Dave, 3
Hepburn, Katharine, 9
Herold, Don, 70
Humphrey, Hubert H., 37
Jackson, Ellen, 73
Johnson, Eric W., 69
Johnson, Lyndon B., 44
Jong, Erica, 83
Jordan, Diana and Paul Seaburn, 8

Kaufman, Max, 12
Kierkegaard, Soren, 12
King, Alan, 48
Kinsey, Mrs. Alfred, 54
Kleinhenz, Sydnie Meltzer, 53
Kohl, Joe, 33, 67
Koren, 60
Kuhn, Clifforn, 63
Landers, Ann, 59
Lansky, Bruce, 30, 34, 43, 46, 48, 49, 51, 66, 74, 76, 99
Lawrence, Bill, 75
Leifer, Carol, 54
Lerner, Alan Jay, 18, 24
Mancroft, Lord, 23
Marvin, Jean H., 62
Marx, Groucho, 61
Mason, Jackie, 95
Maugham, W. Somerset, 49
McGee, Molly, 87
Meltzer, Charlene, 26
Mencken, H.L., 36
Midler, Bette, 59
Milner, Anita, 36
Mirachi, Joe, 28
Montaigne, 71

Montana, Gladiola and Texas Bix Bender, 8
Muehl, Lois, 62
Munro, H.H., 90
Musselman, M. M., 5
Nash, Ogden, 40, 71
Opie, 101
Orben, Robert, 63, 81, 87, 89
Parker, Dorothy, 90
Pearl, Minnie, 11
Peters, Lawrence J., 31
Priestley, J.B., 76
Quitard, 83
Rivers, Joan, 39, 64
Rooney, Mickey, 100
Roseanne, 29, 61, 64, 89
Rowland, Helen, 42, 43
Rudner, Rita, 7, 16, 49, 51, 89
Sather, Drake, 19
Savannah, Susan, 9, 91
Schumann, Robert, 7
Schwadron, 79
Seaburn, Paul and Diana Jordan, 8
Seinfeld, Jerry, 17, 91
Shandling, Garry, 53
Shaw, George Bernard, 74
Simon, Neil, 95

Skelton, Red, 47, 99
Smirnoff, Yakov, 16
Socrates, 12
St. Johns, Adela Rodgers, 31
Steinem, Gloria, 25
Stilson, Jeff, 25
Streisand, Barbra, 68
Thatcher, Dennis, 68
Trevino, Lee, 94
Trillin, Calvin, 70
Tucket, Nan, 32, 64, 77
Turner, Lana, 10
Vagabonds, The, 70
Vass, Susan, 103
Vey, P. C., 57
Vietor, 21
Wambaugh, Joseph, 58
West, Mae, 2, 8
Wilson, Earl, 92
Winstead, Lizz, 1
Winters, Shelly, 7
Youngman, Henny, 5, 20, 22, 39, 41, 52, 65, 86, 92, 102
Zangwill, Israel, 22
Ziegler, Jack, 6, 14, 72

Order Form

Qty.	Title	Author	Order #	Unit Cost (U.S. $)	Total
	Age Happens	Lansky, B.	4025	$7.00	
	Best Baby Shower Book	Cooke, C.	1239	$7.00	
	Best Party Book	Warner, P.	6089	$8.00	
	Best Wedding Shower Book	Cooke, C.	6059	$7.00	
	Dads Say the Dumbest Things!	Lansky/Jones	4220	$6.00	
	Familiarity Breeds Children	Lansky, B.	4015	$7.00	
	For Better And For Worse	Lansky, B.	4000	$7.00	
	Golf: It's Just a Game!	Lansky, B.	4035	$7.00	
	Grandma Knows Best	McBride, M.	4009	$7.00	
	How to Survive Your 40th Birthday	Dodds, B.	4260	$6.00	
	If We'd Wanted Quiet/Poems for Parents	Lansky, B.	3505	$12.00	
	Joy of Friendship	Scotellaro, R.	3506	$7.00	
	Joy of Grandparenting	Sherins/Holleman	3502	$7.00	
	Joy of Marriage	Dodds, M. & B.	3504	$7.00	
	Joy of Parenthood	Blaustone, J.	3500	$7.00	
	Lovesick	Lansky, B.	4045	$7.00	
	Moms Say the Funniest Things!	Lansky, B.	4280	$6.00	
				Subtotal	
		Shipping and Handling (see below)			
		MN residents add 6.5% sales tax			
				Total	

YES! Please send me the books indicated above. Add $2.00 shipping and handling for the first book and 50¢ for each additional book. Add $2.50 to total for books shipped to Canada. Overseas postage will be billed. Allow up to four weeks for delivery. Send check or money order payable to Meadowbrook Press. No cash or C.O.D.'s, please. Prices subject to change without notice. **Quantity discounts available upon request.**

Send book(s) to:

Name_____ Address _____

City_____ State ___ Zip _____ Telephone (____) _____

P.O. number (if necessary) ____ Payment via: ❑ Check or money order payable to Meadowbrook Press

Amount enclosed $ _____ ❑ Visa ❑ MasterCard (for orders over $10.00 only)

Account # _____ Signature _____ Exp. Date _____

A *FREE* Meadowbrook Press catalog is available upon request.

Mail to: Meadowbrook Press
5451 Smetana Drive, Minnetonka, MN 55343

Phone (612) 930-1100   Toll-Free 1-800-338-2232   Fax (612) 930-1940